Gathering Ev

From airbowing in second violins ~~ ... ~~ e mountains to playing poker with nuclear physicists, Caoilinn Hughes finds poems in unexpected places and situations. After gaining BA and MA degrees from the Queen's University of Belfast, she moved to New Zealand. Following some years working for Google, running a small business and writing novels at t weekends, she enrolled to study for a PhD at Victoria University of W gton. Hughes won the 2012 Patrick Kavanagh Award with a selec- t the poems included in this book, and poems from the collection also v e 2013 Cúirt New Writing Prize, the 2012 STA Travel Writing Prize a e 2013 Trócaire/Poetry Ireland Competition.

CAOILINN HUGHES

Gathering Evidence

CARCANET

First published in Great Britain in 2014 by
Carcanet Press Limited
Alliance House
Cross Street
Manchester M2 7AQ

www.carcanet.co.uk

Copyright © Caoilinn Hughes 2014

A CIP catalogue record for this book is available from the British Library

ISBN 978 1 84777 262 6

The publisher acknowledges financial assistance from Arts Council England

 Supported by
ARTS COUNCIL
ENGLAND

Typeset by XL Publishing Services, Exmouth
Printed and bound in England by SRP Ltd, Exeter

for my folks

Acknowledgements

Thanks are due to the following journals and magazines, where some of these poems have appeared: *Aesthetica, The Cúirt Review, Fortnight, The Irish Times, JAAM, Landfall, New Zealand Books, PN Review, Poetry Ireland Review, Poetry New Zealand, Poetry Proper, Poetry Wales, Southword, The Ulster Tattler,* and *The Yellow Nib.* Some poems from the collection were anthologised in *Incertus* (Netherlea Press, 2006) and *Tide Lines* (Queen's University Press, 2005).

'Bolivian Children' won the 2013 Poetry Ireland/Trócaire Poetry Competition. 'Rational Dress', 'Two Roundelets' and 'Airbowing in Second Violins' won the 2013 Cúirt New Writing Prize. 'A Peruvian Blockade According to Bolivia' won the 2012 STA Travel Writing Prize.

A selection of twenty of the poems from this book won the 2012 Patrick Kavanagh Award.

Contents

Avalanche

When the avalanche came down on us

it did not come down on us in a holy light,
flickering between this dimension and another

ultraviolet one. It did not shower its sermon upon us
in meaning-ful, vowel-less sounds like stalactites.
It did not come down on us at all. It came up, up, over

and around us; all around us in a pall. It met our bodies
in a hail, hail, hail, not a wall but heavier than water
if we were sitting at the bottom of the sea. We heard it crack
and sizzle on the ground. It filled the valley like a steam engine;

its clotted vapour urging forward to some terminus beyond us.
We watched it soar and could not inhale enough air between
the screams. Our lungs made fists. I thought of lips freezing shut
once and for all, the uncommon cold, no human fingers to close
the lids nor chance of rescuing the bodies, stiff as candy canes

striped red, white, red, white, grey. Your hands were fifty feet away,
your mind another hundred. My cries could not contend with this parade
of physics. You were wordless, as if the snow were slow motion surf
or a weir devouring its atmosphere. Was it fluid dynamics, glaciology
or meteorology you surveyed? There was something of the shock
wave about it, no doubt about that. The space between us

prolonged. I should never have collapsed in love with a physicist.
I saw the fort my brother built from bales of hay, whose tunnel
should never have been trusted. Oh, to make a hay citadel!
'When the fields are white with daisies,' my father would have said.
The ice wave rose and darkness fell. I doubted how well my elbows
would act as pick-axes, if it were to be a catacomb. I had once been told
that knowing which way is up is key: that the whiteness is homogeneous;
that people dig madly, burying themselves in the immortal white. I panicked:
would he have a better chance than I, with his gall; his practicality?
No, the snow was nothing like confetti. It would not applaud any small boys
or any small girls, no matter how insolent. We braced ourselves, finally.

11

Later, you described the form of a loose snow avalanche as a teardrop;
born of some great disparity between the tensile gift of snow layers
and their compressive heft. The angle of repose was soft, you allowed,
as we stood in the catchment area, making observations and vowel sounds.

Gathering Evidence

He would have been a fan of Newton, the householder
who guzzled his millet gruel and malt beer one bitter
morning in Wales and ran outside to capture hailstones.

'An extraordinary Shower of Hail,' he recorded, 'broke down
the stalks of all the beans and wheat… and ruined as much glass
at Major Hansbury's House as cost 4 pounds the repairing.'

'Some of the Hail were 8 inches about; as to their Figure,
very irregular and unconstant, several of the Hail-stones being
compounded, as the Major judged, who saw them.'

He wore nothing more than rhinegrave breeches
gathered at the knee, garterless stockings, vestless
but for a ruffled shirt – slashed sleeves furled, meaning business.

Gravity had been newly named, so he willed himself to see
the hail as being drawn, not thrown forcefully from the Heavens.
The orbs burst on the ground like meteors or fleshy white melons.

To measure their diameter before they dissolve is to grasp
the hard idea before the thawing thought, he held. If he could secure
a hailstone in a wheelbarrow, with solid algebra, he could square a circle.

To square a circle! He might as well have measured the Garden
of Eden if he could master this binomial expansion. He handled
the pellets like enormous diamonds: what could they reveal? The world

was so full of revelation in those days. One could drop a needle
in a haystack and pinpoint the magnetic field. One could begin a conversation.
He looked at the frozen rain and saw concentric rings as in an axed tree;

he swallowed one like a lozenge, half-hoping a golden band would be left
on his tongue, half-not. His wife pleaded him in to safety. He was ecstatic.
He bellowed how the stones had wed through their seven-mile drop.

What did that mean? His evidence was dissolving; the ghoulish green sky,
lightening. He had not been stunned. He had felt the world upon him,
but the welts it left would not be proof enough. As the Major judged,

if the fellow could only have captured a skyful, he could have squared it.
The esteemed witness was vital. Else, all he would have been
left with was a wife who would not nurse his fever, and indefinite vital signs.

The Transit of Venus

They will lift their pencils and angle them like life drawers,
sizing up Venus against Sol with abstract sums, stiff deductions.

They may see the lead and sniff at how far we have arisen.
They may see and sigh at the recursion. A sun is a sun is a sun.

The telescope is a spyglass into the future, into the slip of the past;
filtering out strata – the lustre that would insult the vitreous mass.

They will watch the brave black circle coming into prospect,
slipping into the bull ring of incandescence, at 3.846×10^{26} watts.

By optical device, they will learn that lead would melt on Venus;
that H_2SO_4 spells neither Hello nor SOS. A salute to Helios?

They will recoil to crows in cornfields, witches on straw brooms,
Tintin, perhaps, the relapse of the Earth to aphelion, the grinning moon.

They will contend with the hundred and fifty million kilometre void;
the inbetween of centaurs, bullion meteors, trojans, asteroids.

They will imagine being James Cook rounding the bravura bend
of Tolaga Bay with its hard-wearing people, its unpolluted sands;

shaking hands with Tupaea, or pressing noses – who knows? –
trading crops, brushstroke techniques, a woe is a woe is a woe;

meeting the far removed tangata whenua, agreeing on the beauty
of the country, the plants, the splendour of astronomy, the mortal duty

to understand the recurring error, hold the warning in their hands:
to persevere with the endeavour to bridge the long, reluctant lands.

Pacific Rim

Since moving further along the Pacific Rim,
I've been waiting for the ground to get a shiver down its spine;
a bit of lust perhaps for the heat at the centre of the earth.
It is more disconcerting than geologically interesting:

not the likelihood that the room will shudder, give way,
quaver (which is more fearsome and frantic than quarter beat
rhythms, I believe what they say), but the anticipation
and possibly unwarranted dread weigh of granite.

It might as well be the twelfth of July in Antrim
with the prospect of pent-up bonfires and reactionary teenagers
spitting beneath their hoods around every unsafe corner, flicking
fag stubs at teenage mums enjoying the smell of petrol
and the orange-coloured blaze a little too intimately.

Police vans with their implied apocalypse, unoccupied cages,
batons swinging by their hips, are almost as threatening.
Reverberations Past might as well be hovering
like knockabout poltergeists graffitiing the ruptured pavements
with convoluted rebellion like palimpsests like prayers however grim.

Children lose their footing, crying: 'Pop goes the ceiling';
cathedrals spill their bricks of hymn upon their neighbours;
flags drop to their knees; gardens split like freshly baked loaves.
The thundering ground, fissuring walls, the sound of history's footfalls.

The Moon Should Be Turned

The cells that were scraped and cut from her
beleaguered cervix – permission neither required
nor sought – were no longer, the court ruled, her belongings.
Flesh could be dissevered and commercialised at will.

Put this specimen into culture, then take your sterile scalpels to the tumor tissue.
Add so many drops of chicken plasma. Lo and behold immortality!

Henrietta's weren't *any* cells: they were dark marvels,
endlessly dividing and swelling like so much yeast.
The Petri dish was no substitute for tableware,
but her martyrdom was fish and bread and butter, if unwitting.

When it comes to cancer cells, there's pretty nearly no products –
other than bullets – that work so well on all people.

Lacks died by the cell that reached the uterus, spleen, lung;
that got so far as Moscow, if not the moon; that contaminated
the heart cells of white men; that was found in the pipe-
dreams of physicians who hoped to smoke out its truth.

The amount of money being spent on medical research, well, it's just piddling.
You won't believe this: less is spent on cancer research than on chewing gum.

However durable, prolific, HeLa cells were political.
They had to make campaign promises. Nixon declared
A War on Cancer, to Culminate in Complete Control; Conquer Death,
which was named a virus. HeLa cells would be its soldiers.

The time has come, in America, when the same concentrated effort that split the atom,
and took man to the moon, should be turned toward conquering this dread disease.

Though the battle wasn't won, Lacks was named, allowed a headstone.
Her children forgave George Otto Gey, the white pharmaceutical brokers;
forgave some twenty tons of their mother that had been grown,
that was living on outside her body; the hostile culture.

King of the Castle

Chicago Pile – 1

The Russians could not come to terms with its construction
in a 'pumpkin field'. Was this some kind of funniness,
or did it conceal a coded meaning; a low-lying, thick-skinned legion?
They might have imagined a Cinderella coach erupting
in chain reaction at the stroke of midnight –
the order of things irreversibly changed.

It was not a pumpkin field but a squash court
under the derelict Western stands of Stagg Field Stadium
where the pile was built: the Metallurgical Laboratory.
Uranium pellets and graphite bricks were wrought from gold and grind.
American science must have seemed like alchemy:
minuscule neutrons splitting heavier atoms into two.

But Fermi had seen it simply: greater radioactivity
on a wooden tabletop than on his own Italian marble.
He had lunched on its mahogany. Mushrooms. Broccoli.
Meat stew. He ate in moderation, then digested slowly: in his gut
he knew it was hydrogen atoms in the wood that slowed the neutrons.
The math would follow. Okay, he told himself calmly. O.K.

K was the reproduction factor, which must equal more than one
for a chain reaction. This was quite a bending of the spoon
for the Italian, as there is no K in his mother tongue. Only *Chi. Che.*
Who. What. How much would be critical. Laura took his plate away
and mouthed, 'Yasher Koach.' He read: 'The curve is exponential,'
though the arc of lip was not. He put it down to fatigue and axial confines.

Later, he stood on the squash court's balcony, watching the grey
balloon–cloth envelope billow – a cloud obscuring the autumn sun.
It masked the structure of brick and timber that would reinforce
the universe: square at the base, a flattened sphere on top.
He choreographed the pile's construction like a painter basking
in perspective; ordering colours, colourlessness, patient brush strokes.

The paintbrushes were cadmium-coated rods that absorbed the neutrons.
At Fermi's command, withdrawing the rods would increase neutron activity,
causing a self-sustaining chain reaction: an émigré Italian controlling
the energy of the atom; calculating the *chiaroscuro* of the sun.
Re-inserting the rods would dampen the reaction, of course, if his math
were not at odds. If it were, Chicago would blush in solar flare.

As the fissile material approached critical mass, each scientist held air
in his lungs a moment too long. Palms sweated sums of last-minute ink to vapour.
The reactor had neither radiation shielding nor a cooling system.
They had not considered cancer sullying their stomachs like slugs; lymphomas
suckling their spines, lymph nodes; exponential neutrons on their neuron piles.
B^n came to mind. Perhaps Fermi had gauged that the sickness would level off.

The most densely populated region in America was safe in his equation, after all.
The clickety-clicking of counters accelerated as the train approached.
They watched the climbing needle the way Isaac Cline watched the barometer
falling in Galveston: rail lines vanishing like gutter grills in overflow; the self-
contained cyclone of suspense whirling in the eardrum. Everyone clambered
to the second storeys of their minds, boring holes in the floor to allow for flooding.

The clicking steadied and began to slide. 'Let's go to lunch,' Fermi said.
The group felt their stomachs land. He had ordered the hourglass to stop its sand.
There was no pep talk. No one mentioned the hazard. They were back
on the court in no time. Weil withdrew the rod like a stick of dynamite,
though he might have handled it like a hundred thousand sticks of dynamite,
as Fermi gave the nod. 'The trace will climb and climb.'

His fingers operated the slide rule like a surgeon threading an intestine.
The men and woman present were silent in the steady brrrr of revolution.
Grim-faced, Fermi turned the rule and jotted meaning on its ivory backbone.
The balcony purveyors had crowded in to eye the instruments,
craning their necks for the split-historical-second. Had they missed it?
Would it be announced like the time of death or birth in a theatre?

Fermi's face broke into a smile: 'The reaction is self-sustaining.' Applause
upturned hands in hesitation. The palms were wilted. They crackled.
The world's first nuclear chain reactor purred for twenty-eight minutes
before he announced it done. It was a long time to trust in foreign physics;
to witness the canvas of the world stretched until one cannot see where the sky begins.
'O.K. Zip in,' Fermi called to Zinn, who held the emergency rod.

The time was 3:53 p.m. Abruptly, the counters slowed, the pen slid
across the paper in a flattening lifeline. Man had started a nuclear reaction
and had stopped it. It was all over. What had it begun? A phonecall
from Compton to Conant in impromptu code: 'The Italian navigator has landed
in the New World.' Conant: 'How were the natives?' Compton: 'Very friendly.'
They poured Chianti into paper cups and drank solemnly, without toasts.

They drank to success, to hope they were the first to succeed, to sleep.
Little would the Russians know how much could be harvested in a pumpkin field.
A small crew was left to straighten up, lock controls, feel the chill of wine spills
on their lapels. As the group filed out from the West Stands like first-time bettors,
a guard asked Zinn: 'What's going on, Doctor, something happen in there?'
The response might have been: 'Oh, nothing death-defying. A game of dominoes.'

This Is What Makes It Go Bang

Take your fired cases
and place them in the chamber.
Hear the hollow thud.

Insert the decapping rod,
then tap the top to rid spent primer.
You will need a soft-faced mallet,
if you can acquire one.

Insert the case, deprimed,
into the body of the dye.
Hammer so the case seats flush.
The body of the case should be fire-
formed to the chamber, should be fire-
formed for truthfulness.

Insert a primer to the chamber.
Place the case, still in the dye,
into the chamber after.
Insert the priming rod, then tap the top.
Do this on a solid surface.
One in every thousand rounds or so,
one in every thousand will go off.
Wear eye protection. If desired, gloves.

Put the primed case, still in the dye,
in the decapping chamber.
Then tap the top to knock the case loose
in the dye. Hear it drop.
The case still in the dye
and decapping chamber,
add your chosen powder.
Use a funnel to pour,
so as not to spill.
So as not to squander.

The case still in the dye
and decapping chamber,
insert your chosen bullet,
be it brass or bullion. More likely
lead alloy with antimony.
Soft-pointed, boat-tailed
for less acrimony.

The case still in the dye
and decapping chamber,
insert the handle of the mallet
then tap the top to seat the bullet.
See that it's snug as an ink cartridge
in a fountain pen.

'Make of it what you will,'
one man instructs another
sitting on spread tabloid,
newsprint and primer on his thumbs.
Tomorrow, they will hunt
bare wither, flank, tree branch
antler, brawny shoulder.

The one who educates leans forward.
He already plans to conceal
the sound of their approach;
to hide the gamey flavour
in smoked venison roast, bacon-wrapped
tenderloin medallions, meatloaf.
He knows how to exploit
the potential of the earth
with gunpowder and curry powder.
He has patience to braise,
broil, poach; to bond the bitter acids
by soaking in buttermilk.

The pupil listens to the instruction.
He leans on the soft-faced mallet
like a crutch. He tells himself to shoulder
the occasion; to drop the case into the body
of the dye; to hammer
so the case seats flush.
One in every thousand rounds
is few and far between.
He practises long silences.
Spills concentrate.

He hammers so the lean cheeks flush:
they are fire-formed for truthfulness.
Hear the hollow thud.

Catechism

Imagine sets of knees aching over the long Rosary,
praying for the conversion of Russia with glassy beads.

My aunt cried 'Up the Reds!' between Hail Marys
and was sent to bed. It might have been half-deliberate

when she snagged the sacrament, launching Glory Bes
into the gluey hives and trenches of her head,

never to be recovered. The floor cannot be knelt spotless.
The confetti falling from skies is shards of anklebone,

flickers of Phantom, the fragile metal feathers of an Albatros.
What is this moral, she might have pled, that draws us in –

like the bead to the stricture of its thread –
like the inevitable torso to the gleaming sword.

Rational Dress

for Marie & Pierre Curie

They took their honeymoon on bicycles;
she in 'rational dress' of bloomers, shirtwaist, linen washing hat;
he in modest-shouldered blazer, silk four-in-hand, love.
'Don't wear laced boots,' the newspaper cautioned.
Don't wear long hued leggings, man's cap, tight garter,
white kid glove or have your golden hair hanging down your back.

'Don't without a needle, thread and thimble.'
It didn't mention beaker, Erlenmeyer flask, dropper pipette,
electrometer, burette, evaporating dish, common sense.
Wed by natural science and civil union, Marie accepted Jesus
lost, along with her mother and sister to typhus. Taciturn condition.
She needn't have read: 'Don't go to church in your bicycle costume.'

She wore her dark blue wedding dress for years on end
in the shed laboratory – once medical dissecting room –
at *l'École Supérieure*, filling its pockets with painstaking findings.
Seeing her brilliance, Pierre left his crystals behind to assist
the weighing out and grinding of pitchblende and chalcolie
with a pestle and mortar – unaware that the diamond they sought

was not a diamond but a needle, which could not be found
in 100 grammes of haystack but in tons of ore. 'Don't undertake a long ride
if you are not confident of performing it easily,' woman had been warned.
All the same, Marie spent long days and nights aglow
in the luminous silhouettes of test tubes, the blue-green activity
of uranium compounds; absorbed in the electric assay of the atom,

wherein she supposed a kind of growth: not a reaction of one thing
with another, but the thing itself dividing into rays like clouds
mushrooming and breaking apart – a culture surging at the heart.
In this fashion, one dawn so cold her dress collar stiffened
to upholstery, she discovered polonium, named after her motherland;
later, pure radium – more powerful still – in between, a daughter: Irene.

'Don't attempt a "century",' the paper opined. 'Don't appear
to be up on "records" and "record smashing." That is sporty.'
On this, society would insist. Pierre had to speak on her behalf
at the Royal Institution, as she sat, hands knotted in the encumbrance
of her skirt. So off the record was she that the Nobel Committee
needed reminding of her work. Was it physics, chemistry or both?

Even still, the record of her body injures: the only woman
interred in the *Panthéon* to stand her own ground.
Her papers, cookbooks, cycling apparel, wedding dress
are stored in lead-lined boxes. To consult them, one must wear
protective clothing. They radiate as if she did not heed the warning:
'Don't scratch a match on the seat of your bloomers.'

On the Content of Brackets

As we watch the seated evening across the field
in all its cool continuance, I imagine what she has missed.
The countless widowed loves she closed her eyes to,
the rumpled linen, train-ride cantos, coastline strolls, missives.
I wonder if there are poppies to spare in Belgium for all this.

She demonstrates age-exemplary patience, coherence,
however convinced it is nineteen-oh-six and nuns are selfish
and male presidents just have more decorum.
The night nurses congratulate her with their lips,
pushing small gratitudes to private guardians.
They unwrap wound dressings like parcels
and remark how well her skin is holding her in.

She tells me the windowsills are brackets,
and only the horizon and its officious moon
can see in and read her: their contents.
I have rarely thought of bracket contents
as being periphery; containing things like flower-
stalks, overlong chapters, rigid bluebottles, Irish,
irrevocable organs, lists.

She counts cattle in the below fields;
plays chess with the evening's reticence.
She has got to eighty-six, as far as the eye can see.

Looting Roses

It is a delicate thing to approach old women
with a wagging finger in a foreign country –
one in particular, woman that is –
telling them not to steal roses.

She turns her face like a library shelf
(all dormant romance and discoloration)
to take me in, in all my nerve
to have ruined a good story.
The thorns in hand are suddenly staged.
But I am not the Queen of Hearts,
outraged and fingering for wet paint;
and it is *not* a good story, I berate,
to have cut those rose heads off at the neck
in however narrow daylight.
Now is not the time to remember
the full minute of consciousness
said to follow beheading. The frown line
feels like full-force riot armour.

It is as appalling a story as the disenfranchised
pigs attempting to overthrow the farm;
looting the barn for muck and Apples.
It is grim as that entitlement and worse perhaps,
since roses don't arrive by way of conveyor belt,
but by time, bruised knee, love-labour.
The left stems are like torn nails too:
rough and threatening to rip apart
the fleece of social order.

Vagabond Monologue

'Funny taste in my mouth. Like… soap. SSS-OW-OO-OA-AH-P! Pah!'

A passerby passes by pronouncing: 'You wouldn't know the meaning of the word, Sir.' He drops a cloudy silver coin onto the asphalt like a hailstone.

'Sir! Kind Sir. Pah!' the vagrant says to himself, livid. Later, his charcoal drawing face changes its composition. The red biro eyes seep:

'I do wonder about this Sir, about this Pah!nsey in his finery and who he might mean to be with his coins clinking by his cock. You can't *be* somebody without meaning to be them. It's a choice they say, the ones with the coins: "you have all the clout in the world with your choices." Pah!

'Like the Sir with his sharp little hips. His tight little lips! Ah-ha-ha! They do say! They do say! Ah yes, the more you say, the more you choose to say. And oh-ho-ho if I could choose to say something! If I still have wheeze in me lungs, juice in me guts I could say fine poetry I tell you. Fine poems you'd mistake for Keats. The Sir himself would say: "Is that Shelley? Is that Eliot? Oh how poignant! How splendid coming from yourself have some soap to wash your mouth out. Have some soap and see if the poetry doesn't flow easier."

'Tell you what makes poetry flow? Nice big bank notes to be writing poems on. Coins are no good for poems. Go away with your soap.'

Snake Creeps through the Grass

The characters seem staged: a businessman swallowing a crustless
sandwich, flaunting his close-fitting skin and rugby-ball cufflinks;
two young ladies with thick lace tights like curtains waiting
to be pulled apart beneath their crushed velvet
dresses and shallow breathing; the beggar-victim
with a beard reddened by weather, fury, Oranjeboom; me.

We stand in the park beside a group practising Tai Chi
to consider the motives of the brat who stole the beggar's beanie.
It seems like a modern-day musical, we agree: 'Rich kid steals
fetid hat with one dollar sixty in copper condolences.'
The beggar declares: 'Insanity! Anarchy! Jealousy! That hat
was worth more than money. To hell with him! The cunt.'

Sensei dip into 'snake creeps through the grass'
interpretatively. I wonder what the vagrant makes of them.
That they are taking up more than their share of oxygen, maybe?
I confirm the cunt-thief was twenty-something and sporting
brand-new faded jeans. His hair flopped open on his head
like a dead butterfly. I don't describe how it gleamed.

I don't point out that the Tai Chis did nothing to intervene;
that their 'cloud hands' seemed to wave the thief off lovingly.

The Shell Man

''S'my birthday too,' he said, tinkling the piano keys of his teeth. 'Feelin' dat salt-sweet nostalgia. She a scorpion. You sound though you should be homesick. You feelin' good? You's young. You gots dese friends here. Da's more'n I got. Girl I show you a trick for yo birthday. Fo both our birthday. But you gotta bet a buck. Can't do without no buck.'

The bus hisses, pulls away. The wallet in my lap is full of thrift store promises, fake I.D., stamps, a graph of numerical compatibility, teenage cult, lyrics that won't be put to music.

'You is Irish. Dem's the lucky ones, right? Dem's the cloverleaf eatin' type, am I right? Say Irish gots all the luck. I got me *Frisco Weekly*, ain't nothin' to write home tell. No good news nohow. Here we goin' fold dis newspaper, lay out dese shells and I'ma goin' do dat Irish dancin' right here. Goin' shuffle me some shells. You gots to watch where de pea go. You gots young eyes, blue like the sea where dem shells be, so folla it good now. Do your dolla a favor. Watch de pea. We double o' nothin's the rules. Double or nothin' birthday dough. Be bread soon. Dough swell good. We goin' be richer dan butter melt on dat bread. Da's how de Irish goin' jack Ingelendtown, by doubling dem dollas. Gets dey own land back. De help o'God. Show me you mean bi'nis. Here we go.'

Friends scan the aisle, swallow hard. 'Say no?' Passengers gaze out the window, hard. One frowns, shakes her head so her short grey hairs float like wishless dandelion clock like banknotes. Another observes the bottlecaps, age-old discourse.

'Yo mind tied up, s'why you lose. Be wishin' for some birthday present nobody buy you? Folla de pea, win yo money back, buy yo own self souvenir. Double it up now, where it at?'

He reaches for my wallet, then the pullcord. A man in a Giants hat gestures to the third bottlecap. His eyes implore.

'Gotta hustle. Need yo bread. Need yo cheddar come chowtime. Be hungry in dem long summer days, but you know none o' dat hunger. Famine be history in yo town. Yo pop got bank. How I see it. Everyday a birthday. Pot fulla gold be at de end o' all dem rainbows, an' I hears Irish knows how to rain good, see.'

The Giants fan is a shill. He evades so many downcast eyes, it's all he can do to be a shooting star. The shells must hold cartridges, we think. The newspaper is all holes.

'This my stop. My birthday. Irish go hunt 'nother rainbow.'

Somatic Cells

This is the bright side of the world, I tell him.
It is up over. They got it upside down, I avow,
turning the labyrinth of words on their heads
for a better angle on their vowels, on their open
endings. My lover quivers at the tail end of *thwart*
as though it were telling him something;
as though it were really self-contradicting,
but he is trying to draw attention from *rewards*
in the far corner, ready to be plundered
like an under-populated hemisphere.
Wave. Awe. Avow. Ova is 'a haploid female
reproductive gamete'. Somatic cells get
twice as many chromosomes. Haploid females.
Somatic cells. Hapless males. Semiotic girls.
No, for twice as many chromosomes
it's half as many points. I'll withhold the V.
It might have more potential later as a virus
or even as something viscous or vicious, if I happen
to acquire the elusive S and could double it
O what happiness. He turns a blank piece of pine
over and back across his lifeline.
Someone has scribbled an S upon it in blue biro
like the vein of a wrist, but it is not legitimate.
The Scrabble board is a globe and you and I
are toying with varying degrees of latitude.

Impressions of Ireland

New Zealanders have been telling me of home and times gone:
the tense most accustomed to the tongue in Ireland.
They visited counties, they announce, like Old Testament Gospels,
which I didn't know had survived beyond history books.

I imagine the counties to be like dusty library copies of *Beowulf*,
spines cracked to smithereens with no one to commiserate
since all the kids who have to read Seamus Heaney translations
on their Kindles, which are not as good for making fires as they sound.

They sum up their impressions of Ireland in consecutive days of rain:
twenty-five-I-reckon-eh, we had forty-one-I-swear-to-Cuchulain,
making up their own mythology with inverted vowel sounds
and shaking their heads for not having enough hands or ribs to count on.

They visited purposefully, they tell me: for the sake of heredity,
however bloodless; to link themselves to a thrice-removed
history, as if their own shades of jade were not as profound,
as if their own peculiarly practical cities – however few and far between –

were no places to be proud of; as if their diversity of skin, of tongue,
of being from islands in the antagonistic Tasman, the defiant Pacific,
were not enough to beget self-esteem. I feel ashamed never
to have read *Beowulf* or walked the Ring of Kerry with all its rain.

To the Elements

It is not the piebald impressionism of the afternoon window
bleeding greys into the hills and gay greens into the thickset heavens
but real rain that dissolves the halo of your hair to show your skull
for what is there. It doesn't wash off sins no matter how you kneel to it.

We grovel to our yellow home, which is not a submarine but a fragile hollow
in the thick surrounding sea. How its carbon backbone does not fracture
under the pressure is unconscionable. It holds us in its collapsible wings
through the mid–winter sundown which is even less forgiving than it sounds.

The rain pours petrol onto our cling film roof, then throws us –
boy and girl and bivouac to boot – into the fire of sunset to hear us erupt.
You sleep directly, grasping for tree branches in your evolutionary dreams.
I lie wakeful, waiting for the enormous harm, which we may or may not overcome.

We Are Experiencing Delay

We are experiencing a delay due to a body on the tracks
the broadcaster drones. Fluid pools in lower limbs that have been disowned.
A body is experiencing delay among the ballast and the black.

We throttle our tabloids like pillowcases, as if to rid the newscasts
of their creases, though headlines cannot compete with the coroner megaphone.
We are experiencing delay due to a body on the tracks.

No one is reading a love letter behind a Henry James hardback.
Neither sympathies, books nor lovers have been taken out on loan.
A body is experiencing delay among the ballast and the black.

Aside sleepers, we search Perseus's shield for cracks:
we see our sorry forms in darkened perspex. We are not as we are shown.
We are experiencing delay due to a body on the tracks.

Home is an idea that comes and goes. The idea is carried on our backs;
now silk-lined, now boned. All there is of its embodiment are steppingstones.
A body is experiencing delay among the ballast and the black.

There will be no tombstone in the landscape for a page marker, for a fact.
The speaker intones: *We will not be long.* Headlines, epitaphs: He is not alone.
We are experiencing a delay due to a body on the tracks.
A body is experiencing delay among the ballast and the black.

Two Roundelets

I

regarding love:
the gift is an hourglass, turned.
Regarding love,
its leaking silts are gilings of
unhandled skin, inhaled commands.
I gauge the slip, the guilt of sand,
regarding love.

II

regarding time:
heat escapes our teacups, disbands.
(Regarding time,
we neglect the elemental.)
Noughts stain my writing desk, distend.
Our heat cannot be reconciled,
regarding time.

Every Body Continues In Its State Of Rest

Day one of six, you're having mechanical issues.
'Jockey wheel's chewed up. Damn rear derailleurs. Where's the mettle?'
Your bike won't let you crossgear to chase me up a hill
to be the first to see the Tasman. (We are fresh-limbed;
bull-willed.) You have to work your way up, cog by cog. This is fair.

The pannier bags are doughy backsides waggling. They are equal
and opposite to our Daedalian bodies. We equipoise the question
of feather versus carbon crankshaft, hammer versus asphalt gradient,
drag coefficient as opposed to Kevlar purchase: the acceleration
is inversely proportional to the mass of the frame. This is tedious.

We are a pair of lunatics, we are repeatedly informed, seesawing
the extremes of bliss and agony, blood and sugar, natural beauty
and freight traffic. We push the road behind us so that we might outpace
our calendars. We make 'lifecycle' jokes. Eight hundred kilometres
is enough to talk ourselves tyre-flat, saddle-sore. This is inertia.

The pollen in so many cubic metres of countryside is countless.
I sense you fall back from the joy of it: the theoretic physics of the peloton.
Head down, heart-rate constant, *One Square Meals* clogging in your gut.
You note placenames like a bibliography: We have been here, we will go there.
In between, there may be photo opportunities, subject to punctures. This is fatigue.

Mauve doesn't suit my buttocks, you say, let alone crust. Let's hitchhike.
'Are you done?' You shrug the oil-stained condor shoulders – the bastard wings
we have developed. The velocity is fitful. We violate the conservation of spirit.
Our itinerary is not a closed system. I fight the damp nor'wester; pry apart a slipstream.
'Come draft off me.' I grimace. It's the pollen, you say, eyes streaming. This
                                                                    is endurance.

Lucky

I sit on the rain-coloured carpet at the foot of the bed, feet tucked under an oil heater.
You don't see the goosepimples prove where my dressing gown parts.
You're reading *Waiting for Godot* for the first time. It feels like an occasion.

You demand: What's the meaning of this?
Lucky's speech. Logorrhea?

The one about God and depravity and tennis?
I don't remember. Give me the gist.

You say: That's the pickle. Can't.

If… you read it aloud, I'll… love you for it, I suggest, demoting Kipling to my lap.
I blink conjunctivitis. You lay into it. Goosepimples demand attention.
You finish, short of breath. I twist, grinning madly.

You say: Don't get it.

Nor I, but stand up, signalling madly.
My skull is doing its own thing, pulling the body after it. I fret it might detach.
You haul back my reckless brain cells by your reasoning. Neurons curtsey.

You point to the window, where the curtain is parted like a sideways eyelid,
pretending to be asleep. Our neighbour is watching us: the meaning of life laid bare.
The gown has come undone and goosepimples are everywhere. I curtsey.

You say: I should be so Lucky.

Marbles

A netted bag of green glass marbles with aquamarine swirls
deep in the otherworld of spherical transparency (simultaneous opacity)
was the first thing I ever stole when I was three and far from the last.
The marbles hung heavily in their lattice like motherless pearls,
like lifeless organs in between bodies, intervening worlds.

I gave them the damp of my palm, envisioning the cold shell nurture
of dinosaur eggs or black hole ovule. When I had lost each glass orb,
I filled my pockets with millefiori beads, Bangladeshi bracelets, Electric Eel
eye-shadow, neon ping-pong balls. But nothing weighed the same as the
                                                                stolen marbles
that gave me unbuyable glee and bellyaches when I swallowed them experimentally.

Communion Afternoon

I would have outsmarted them or, at a minimum,
flicked their coins back like sharp-edged playing
cards or swung the rosary beads like a Filipino Balisong
had I not vomited spaghetti alphabet all over the spring-time
grass and fake-white silk and girlhood; disgusted
at the injustice of being small and atheist and inarticulate.

Cynophobia

It did not start when my brother held his face in his palms
like a shredded piñata. Even before that mess of rubicund
flesh, I was scared of them. I could not come to his aid for dread.

It was not a sin but a precaution: the private war-drum of palpitation;
fizzing sweat glands portending chemical warfare; oesophagus closing in on itself
to the size of a straw; tongue parching to blotting paper, drawing out the nerve.

It was our Aunt's Alsatian that attacked: its ancestral wolf sensed a threat,
brought its paws to the plastic gunfight my brother and cousin enacted.
Bang, bang, you're dead had real-life, bacteria-lined effect.

'Cowering on the ground and urinating oneself is advisable,' a postwoman told me,
if one encounters a Rottweiler – accidentally encroaches upon its postbox kingdom.
I would have told my brother, but his ears were gory. His vocabulary was limited.

Dogs like that can sense tension around the commissures, in the buttocks,
the suppressed syllable; that I am neat-limbed, thin-wristed; that all my bones
are perfectly intact; that they are soft and susceptible to teeth as bullion.

Once the mutt has got the better of me, I like to think of my brains
as a pomegranate: drought-tolerant, widely cultivated, packed with seeds
embedded in spongy pulp membranes – a grenade in its possessive gut.

It started when my mother dropped me off at driveway's end in a rush.
Birthday candles blinked from a distant window: someone else's wish took flight.
It started then, between a black Labrador and a locked door: the
                                          extinguished lights.

Playing House

They sprinkle sugar over ice cubes;
transform plastic into porcelain
with pinkie fingers and lifted chins.

The girls invent us as we go along.
I force sense back into its box.
Fool myself silly.

I am told I have set a bomb
in their sandmade city
and now I must defuse it.

I don't know how to defuse a bomb.
Distant London buses drone
in the thumping distrust.

One lets her chin drop.
The other, her small finger. Already,
they know far too much of human nature.

Dublin Can Be Heaven

She used words like haberdashery casually
in conversation while playing out anagrams on our backs
with affectionate fingertips. The same pin-prinked fingertips
that on occasional winter mornings would thrum hot air
out of our duvets at six a.m. in the navy of sleep,
whispering a familiar tune to explain the too-soon wakening;
spreading butter on our breakfast of consciousness,
d'care would we use a knife, however rounded.

Dublin can be heaven, with coffee at eleven
and a stroll down Stephen's Green…
The song was for just us two, so she sang subdued
like faraway vinyl and without vibrato.
From the bed across the room my sister groaned,
There's no need to hurry, there's no need to worry
through the pillow safeguard and she would grin:

'But we should hurry loves, to catch the early train.'
The train to Dublin with our mother on a school day.
The train with our mother who wrote spurious sick notes;
who cut off her plait at the nape of the neck like a rope,
resigned it to the top drawer with the patterned silver
and wouldn't forgive us for doing the same; who likened
the world to a stage, past loves to Thee Doctor Fell with his cape.

We drank coffee in carriage two, dropping in cream
and watching it plume. We scooped out the nectarines
of hand-me-down lipsticks, convinced of the romance
of orange-lipped adulthood when *we* could sneak our daughters
out of school and onto trains with paper cups and fountain pens,
so they could watch their mother's gold-dust hair
and crossword concentration and pretend to chew on nine across,
desperate to disguise the childish signs of happiness.

Hames of a Haiku

Two biddies on a train discussing a poorly taken photograph with Our Lady of Lourdes.

'The photographer cut
off our hats and – imagine –
Our Lady's halo.'

'We had the frame bought
and all. Now what? Demote Her
to the family scrapbook?'

'You get these chances
once in a blue… bloody well
blasphemous it was.'

Soldiers in the Battle for Hedonism

You make D9 with your thumb as though the chord is a torn muscle:
if you hold the dissonant strings at length they will re-thread.
I don't offer rest as the best remedy. Instead, I leaf through poetry volumes,
squinting for hidden flick-book drawings in the broken black shapes.
There are none, so I compare Mahon and Morrissey to Keats and Shelley
and try to find assonance. It is more visceral in the Irish. It is more sharply
angled: the vowels are bicycle spokes, gyratory; aslant for an ankle –
the vulnerable malleolus – to shred. I push aside the slender spectres
and they slip off one other like egg yolks or silk scarves or envelopes.
'How has life really changed for people like us?' I digress to dialogue,

holding *Observe the Sons of Ulster Marching Towards the Somme* lightly
and wondering what you could possibly know about it. You play
the paradox of bluegrass and explain to me: 'Food is less of a factor now.
Say what you like about battery farming. We're worse off for our homes, but.
And getting from A to B is quick but costly. Plus, our ravenous bodies
go on and on and there's no sponge like old skin, I'll tell you that for free.
Our taste buds have turned to custard. Our vocabulary is stiff as schoolboys'
socks and there's more where that came from. We're more full
and more wanting than ever. To people like us, C major is caustic.
We are soldiers in the battle for hedonism, to put it like your poetry.'

Atmospheric Physicist vs Poetic Atmosphericist

You send sound signals into the atmosphere
and listen for how they return, distorted.
You measure turbulence – one of the last things
we're willing to say is unsolvable.
Deciphering the data and gathering
inference is how you stay alive.

I send sound signals into the atmosphere
and listen for how they return, distorted.
I measure turbulence – one of the last things
we're willing to say is unsolvable.
Gathering the data and deciphering
inference is how I stay alive.

Estuary

Our arms are full of other people's babies: the shapeless
oyster fleshes of becoming. Nucleotides flood our laps, girdle
our wrists. Our mouths are full of cooing, cawing serenade.
'A pearl,' we smile. We must take to this tender pink like tourists,
handling the toss of heads: *how privileged we are we are
we are* so prevailing in our choices. We go shoeless.
We collapse our sneezes into our chests. We do not let on
at the gutters of our bodies – we are hollow gastropod shells.

They observe our course, unfastened hands, whose only charms
are the scars of riverbeds, carnal somersaults, solitaire calluses.
Do we know what lies ahead? All lives come to an estuary,
in time. In their dancing eyes the world contracts to a coil:
a single dark loop quivering like all the bulged lips;
primed to suck, to kiss everybody in.

Bruisewort

I can no longer make a daisy chain that is the sum of its parts.
The joins lack mindlessness. The split stems are DNA strands:
backbones of sugars and phosphates linked by invisible ester bonds
like children's crossed palms, swallowing the weekly good intentions in white

unleavened disks that are neither sugar nor phosphates. They taste of hands.
To discover the atom is a start – to know what it means; its particle trinity
that has oceans cleaving to the tilted earth resisting the moon's recurrent invite;
miraculous photosynthesis, which is bodiless, yet we grope about for its
photon torso.

If I reassess the sum of its parts, does the daisy chain become divinity,
since the electron and its positron hold the pattern of our future infinitesimally?
This is more modellable than we would like to concede. Its Latin name, a propos,
means pretty-everlasting. You could say interminable-beauty, but that is evaluative,

not quantitative; besides, they were once called bruisewort. Names are generally
variable. A daisy chain is not, as the eye would allow, a succession of weeds:
each one is a composite flower, whose petals are not just correlative,
but are individual flowers. Even the yellow centres comprise microscopic flowers.

They are an army of atoms; of would-be flowers working together to spread
the seeds
of their existence. If their astral particles are the emblems of probability,
should we swallow the astringent petals weekly and see what follows?
Ø to know how anti-particles balance the pseudanthium with all its quarks!

With a fast enough machine, we could decode the daisy chain in calculus,
Objective-C,
transcendental equations. Would the parts of its sum be atoms or litanies?

49

Bolivian Children

The children from El Chorro were so much like adults
with their outfits and their hardships; the main distinctions
being bowler hats, stamina, the length of plaits.

They rushed up to examine us, prodding our rucksacks
like alien illnesses with Aymara hecklings and muddy
index fingers: momentary bridges between existences.

I stopped in my tracks to greet them, suddenly foolish
in woollen clothes coloured by the blood of cochineal bugs
and gore and sewn by too-small hands, too much like their own.

Their eyes drew towards an unopened Snickers in my glove
like a love letter – its unseen, foreign parable
might have been so much more than cocoa, sugar, caramel.

I am sure those pieces of our encounter were torn asunder later
by too-small hands, too many muddy fingers waging war
with cochineal blood beneath the nails, and a new taste for wayfarers
who leave nothing but creases in Cholita skirts and sugar-coated leftovers.

A Peruvian Blockade, According to Bolivia

It is something when border towns fill to the brim;
when borders close up and you are shut in
'For good?' 'Just for now,' 'Until news is out,'
'till tomorrow, *mañana, pocito mas tarde*,'
the fishermen say to the townsmen in tongues.
It's a landslide, they tell us; there are men with their backs
bent over like lampposts to shovel it up,
but no one gets through for today, ask tomorrow,
when they say: it's Peru; it's the polls, it's their fault!
It is a country that's utterly falling apart!
Tut tut to Peru, but you cannot get through
but by Chile, *dinero*, long days on a bus.
You'll be sorry tomorrow when it's all in the past.
But for now the *Aduanas* aren't giving out stamps.
The *Carabinieros* are picking their nails
with the corners of passports and wiping their boots
with the cash of the fools who are pitching their tents
on the edge of Peru, with no food now for days
empañadas no water no tomorrow we'll know;
now we know! News is out! It's the miners, you see,
they are worse off than us. It's the miners blockading
and causing the fuss. Get your stamps now, for what?
The roads are all blocked for hundreds of miles,
just imagine the rocks! Bigger than houses
they're blocking the way, *peligrosos incendios*!
Boulders and flames all the road long, and the men
with their belts, *los campesinos borrachos*,
are whipping their rage and their tongues!
They are drunk now for days and angry and tired
from lugging the rocks. They will not let you through,
not even for favours, not even with luck.
But what luck for the border town, Copacabana
(not the one from the song), when the fishermen's homes
are converted to bars and the tourists are stuck
and are drowning their woes in Pisco and Quilmes
and plentiful bank notes from new leather wallets
with desperate measures and new woollen socks.

Altitude

Huayna Potosí (6,088 m)

We breakfast at midnight; swill Acetazolamide
with coca tea, savouring the narcotic promise.
We chew bread leathery as biltong and the gut
registers its complaint. Temples pulse and swell
like the vocal sacs of frogs: distending for the distress
signal; deflating into inner monologue.

The climb begins at one. Three humans walk in a line:
reticent, breathy, leashed together on a mountain darkened
by the list of the planet and fear of looking into space.
The guide in front is balaclava'd and tired of altitude.
His family is not safe in La Paz. Its houses are lockless.
His wife is anaemic and submissive to strangers.

I think of her dyspnoea and wonder if it is contagious.
In the middle, I am snowed under rented wardrobe. Overdosed
on Diamox, Soroche, Advil (having tried two of each).
Pins and needles fizz from tailbone to tear duct; cheeks moil;
saliva spumes. I don't expect to make the summit, but until
the stomach gives, I measure evolution in footprint glyptics.

You watch the teeth of my heels gouge the ice;
see in my paces the ratio of our lives together: lives apart.
I recall freak placenames learned by heart as a cure for world-
weariness: Burnt Prairie, Constellation, Pencilbluff, Briar,
Buttermilk, Searchlight, Rabbit Hask, Frostproof.
There is a place called Why, I want the energy to tell you.

It is demeaning to have my tracks held out for me; shaming
as childbirth stirrups. I forget how not to move into them,
like truisms or mothers' mannerisms. Every other hour, I sulk,
'I have come far enough.' My padded bottom thumps the snow
in deposition. What a place to sit for sunrise. Teo frowns.
'Hacemos una pausa, y subimos,' he goads us on, lest our sweat glaciates.

In my pack, the camera battery has frozen. Water clatters.
The blood develops alkaline. Again, the mind drifts:
Teo resents us. He imagines how we would make his wife cower;
draw the rare iron out of her like the violent magnets of industry.
Her long-established plaits become tromino tessellations in the trance;
the tongue; the Beckettian rhythm of our tortoise progress.

Six kilometres into the sky, the gloom lifts enough to show
your GPS device. Teo does not pretend to care about our privilege.
To cross an ice shelf, a windowsill, he bolts us to the mountain.
As if tightening the corkscrew neuron, your fear of heights arrives.
I say: Gravity has never let us down. It doesn't demand a leap of faith.
See: the mountain is a perfect wishbone, casting an inverse V

of shadow leagues across the landscape. Peru. Bolivia. Teo's eyes
are thawing in his balaclava. Perhaps he thinks, *Este es mi cielo.*
I want to translate: This is all I know of being a crepuscular creature,
engaged from dusk to dawn; a firefly – only, without the compound eyes
and luciferan abdomen. I cannot take in great landscapes.
No matter how you and I pleat and pack, we are not visible from space.

God Always Geometrises

I measured the skies, now the shadows I measure.
Skybound was the mind, earthbound the body rests.
– Johannes Kepler

He was the first to stare at stars and really dream
of travelling. He gauged the radii between earths
and suns by careful estimation, deduction, thirst
of acumen. Mars was not a Hallowed warning but an Axiom.

He would navigate the Holy Spirit – space – between
God, seated upon Sol, and his Son: the astral musician.
He would bring back to earth a law of motion.
Veritas from Saturn. One must not become a libertine,

his mother warned, when he raved of the sublime
altitudes and began examining metaphysics
through a telescope at eleven, deciphering in the universe
designs far too arithmetical to be divine.

His father fled to the Netherlands, the Eighty Years' War,
never to return; so Katharina Guldenmann nursed
the parts of her son that could carry on fatherless, cursed.
Her shoulders were pilasters of thought. They would endure.

She held young Kepler's wafer frame up to the Great Comet;
to see the lunar eclipse that made the moon appear
reddened. He maddened at its indistinct picture.
His eyes were unreliable. Smallpox had rotted their promise.

It would take his own son by the throat and throttle
the life out of him like the conflict out of a paradox
one day. Then there would follow the sonless equinox.
But before those burdens that awaited him – the chattel

of creed; the death to spotted fever of a twice-widowed wife;
wasted labour; the trial of witchcraft he would bring upon his mother –
before all that strife, he dreamt of interstellar travel; the sonorous ether;
of hearing the harmony of the spheres, at the threshold of afterlife.

Harmony of the Spheres

for Johannes Kepler

Heaven knows the planets are not silent in their orbits.
They sound of swallows making cyclical migrations;
returning blue-feathered, quavering melancholic airs.

Though, Angelic unison is compromised on Earth
for we are not its audience: its song is directed Sun-
ward. A degree of alteration is required for melodic heirs.

Celestial orbs were placed by the Creator to balance
consonance with dissonance; discord with concord:
with each revolution resounds chromatic fanfares.

For the same reason, the seasons turn their backs:
the planets loom and whirl and leave the Sun, Moon, Earth
and we should heed the progression of Apostolic prayers.

The nature of all things observes the geometric compliment.
Even our eyes show the numeric inverse of His
cosmos in their rendering; a Soul therein the optic stares.

Equally, distance, velocity, hastening can be measured
in the triad of our wisdom. Father, Ephemeral Son, swan feather,
telescope: the semitones between us are rhapsodic lairs.

Life on Earth is fleeting, exhausting. Our griefs are swallows
lifting small wing chords. Thus, as passage migrants,
we too play our part in the great symphonic overture.

Airbowing in Second Violins

I hold the horse hair as a swan feather
against the long finger knuckle, balancing its back-
bone on my thumb. The hairs are taut and firm
and one of them is causing pain, but I cannot tell which one.

This rigid catgut will not suffer the ridged E unless it must:
unless I sense an ear aslant; an elbow fold its angle in –
forge bellows' *shush*. Tutting. *Tutti*. We throng together.
B flat major precipitates the unbuckling of backs.

I am exact in my flick of wrist, my grace notes;
like how death is delicate in its tiptoeing among atolls;
its swallowing of atmosphere from black hole stalls, the endless
gallery abyss; the immortal Scherzo demisemiquavers overleaf.

Music is not a love bite on my neck, but the wound of making
no sound (like when I was made to practise with a wooden stick
to understand the gesture better: some Hungarian method I think.
I liked to play that ghostly song; to auscult the belly *f*s.)

The time signature is death's autograph in an orchestra:
nine eighths of threefold trouble. My neighbour gives the death-
stare. *Grave*. The Wolf Tone is inexorable from Irish instruments,
I grovel, roll my head and make of the chin rest a riata.

Watershed

It is the first of spring and I can smell boiling rhubarb
pluming through the kitchen in Knockdoe, and can hear the shush
of popping brushwood from across the simmering margin;
from Belfast's ever-melting hill tops, tarmacadam, dry dock.
I return to hear less undaunted jackdaws, fewer sparrows still.

It is the first of spring and things are seemingly diminishing:
Brazilian grey-winged continga, the African grey parrot,
clouds, pencil lead, simple concrete – possibly all greynesses.
They say pyramids are resilient, so we make turf tents for Napaeae.
Such young plums are picked at home. I see the crows are panicking.

Is It A Kind Of Bell Toll?

The sound that precedes the writing of poems rests upon who
if anyone is there – is here – to hear it occur and whether
they are benevolent jurors; how the room's hollows,
its caverns and cambers, are arranged, if it is a room at all;
if it is not the dell of a tomb or dungeon; if it is not the roaring,
rained-in interior of a Land Rover; if the listeners' perilymphs
are off-kilter: heads tipped like eggs placed carelessly in egg cups.
It is a pity no one treads carefully over eggshells any longer.
It is a pity no one uses ink wells or fountain pens with their vials
of dark blue hypotheticals with their tell-tale owners with their ink-
stained calluses with their bad habits with the tick tick tick
of postponement. And the sound. Is it a kind of bell toll?

For me the outset sound is a *ting* of precious metal instilled
with a bright green amulet – the kind exhumed among the limbs
of Egyptian children wrapped in linen and millennia –
a chrysocolla and sterling silver ring dropped upon a tabletop,
to be specific, some kind of pine draped in a mantle of varnish
and very supportive. This is all part of the ceremony. The readying.
I divest myself of the ring like the world of the living, like an offering,
then perhaps some knuckles rid themselves of their calcium deposits.
At least my knees aren't tucked inside my ribs with the grind
of bone on bone like Incan cadavers or Sophocles' fist on chin.
The endeavour is mostly trivial. The sound is mostly din.

Legacy

'These estates were gambled in a card game in the twenties,'
he tells me; the whole acreage from high ground to flooded turf,
encircling bartizans of pine, maple, oak – centuries in the growing –
as far as the retina can twirl. *Acres for aces* I want to joke.

'Those were the kind of bets that held. No remortgaging.
Losing your fortune meant making a living like everybody else.
Nothing like fierce labour to recede the hairline, widow's peak
and all the glitter thereafter. There were no such things as plugs.'

I consider the menopausal Ant Queen whose fellow Echinatiors
offer not to eat her if she will live as lowly worker.
Not the leaf-cutter caste: she must tend the fungal gardens
meticulously, cultivate the mould, act a kind of dinner-lady.

I follow, obedient, trusting there'll be time and language later
for estranging. We brush off nettled-in cenotaphs; push aside
famine houses' thistle windows; clear out dilapidated Ra shelters
with their obscured watchwords; hide, seek, know atrophy from entropy;

we climb each tor that holds to weather like the registers of Irish history.
The Black & Tans filled their gats with cartilage. Their calloused knuckles
pummelled mandibles like gumboots into a muck of Sundays, into a host of homes.
'Both sides but, more's the pity. Their quarrels were with the world and not
                                                           the self –

the wrong way to have it, as Yeats himself knew well, and he a halfie.'
His eyes are dashes, fragmentary. 'Bloody jailbird-soldiers set alight
these here manors and slit the Fire Brigade's hosepipes with their flick
knives. Call that Good News too, I'll have you know.'

Go on. I draw out what the decades haven't ravaged.
These soliloquys are souterrains. The implication of his talking
is the stone-by-stone construction. He only pauses over dinner tables:
grave silences come of the delicate picking at fish bones.

Boots on again, full-stomached. The cows are roosted, sopping up the long
afternoon like bales of hay. The sound effect is a kettle ever on the boil.
The cattle do not heed the downfall on their pied withers;
the black loam seething, rising all around them like seditious ants.

We will not be put to work or put down or put out of our homes.
His pace quickens. The sharp inhale of breath: *Enough*. Was it?
Or: *Enough's enough*? I stay a foot behind. I time my step
to catch the sentence if it fails; to be in his shadow, if that's the safer place.